Guess What!

Student's Book 2B

Susannah Reed with Kay Bentley
Series Editor: Lesley Koustaff

CAMBRIDGE
UNIVERSITY PRESS

Contents

Meals

Guess What!

1 (CD2 19) Listen. Who's speaking?

2 (CD2 20) Listen, point, and say.

1 potatoes
2 carrots
3 rice
4 peas
5 sausages
6 fish
7 meat
8 beans
9 toast
10 cereal

The Co...
Breakfast 8
Lunch 1
Dinner

3.65

Find Leo

3 (CD2 21) Listen and find.

4 ^{CD2} **Say the chant.**

Do you like toast for breakfast?
Do you like cereal, too?
Toast and cereal for breakfast?
Yum! Yes, I do.

breakfast

lunch

dinner

 5 Think **Read, look, and say. What's missing?**

Shopping list

cereal
sausages
meat
peas
potatoes
beans
rice
fish

Sing the song.

My friend Sammy likes 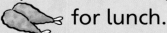 for lunch.
He doesn't like ,
And he doesn't like .
He likes and ,
And he likes .

Munch, Sammy.
Munch your lunch!

My friend Sally likes for lunch.
She doesn't like ,
And she doesn't like .
She likes and ,
And and .

Munch, Sally.
Munch your lunch!

7 CD2 25 **Listen and say _Sammy_ or _Sally_.**

8 About Me **Ask and answer. Then say.**

Do you like fish?

Yes, I do.

Alex likes fish.

9 CD2 27 **Listen, look, and say.**

1

2

10 Think **Ask and answer.**

Tony

Is it a boy or a girl?

It's a boy.

Does he like meat?

Yes, he does.

Does he like carrots?

No, he doesn't.

It's Tony!

Kim

Tom

Pat

→ Workbook page 51

Grammar: *Does he like cereal?* **63**

11 CD2 28 Listen and read.

1

Look! Café Hawaii!

Café Hawaii

Let's go for lunch!

2

Café Hawaii

Would you like fish and potatoes?

Yes, please!

No, thank you!

3

What about carrots or peas, iPal?

No, thank you!

4

Oh, dear! What would you like, iPal?

Cake! I like chocolate cake.

5

More cake, please!

No, iPal.
That's enough!

6

What's the matter?

He likes chocolate cake – a lot!

64 Value: Eat healthy food

→ Workbook page 52

12   **Listen and act.**

Animal sounds

13 (CD2 31) **Listen and say.**

A seal in the sun. A zebra in the zoo.

What kind of **food** is it?

1 🔊 CD2 33 Listen and say.

1

2

3

4

5

fruit   vegetables   meat   grains   dairy

2 Watch the video.

3 Look and say what kind of food it is.

Number 1. Fish.   Yes.

Guess What!

1

2

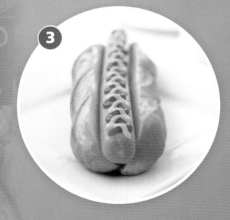
3

4

Project

4 Make a food poster.

6 Activities

Guess What!

1 (CD2 34) **Listen. Who's speaking?**

2 (CD2 35) **Listen, point, and say.**

3 (CD2 36) **Listen and find.**

70 Vocabulary

→ Workbook page 56

4 CD2 37 **Say the chant.**

I can play tennis.
I can't play field hockey.
Let's play tennis.
Good idea!

basketball
baseball

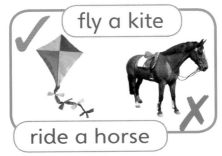
fly a kite
ride a horse

take photographs
roller-skate

 5 About Me **Match and say.**

1, e. I can roller-skate.

1 I can roller-skate.
2 I can take photographs.
3 I can ride a horse.
4 I can play tennis.
5 I can play field hockey.

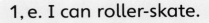

a

b

c

d

e

 6 About Me **Point and tell your friend.**

Picture b. I can play tennis.

Picture e. I can't roller-skate.

7 CD2 39 **Listen, look, and say.**

1 I like playing basketball, I don't like swimming.

2 I like swimming. I don't like playing basketball.

8 CD2 40 **Listen and say the name.**

Ann

Pam

Jack

Bill

Alex

Grace

9 About Me **Things you like. Think and say.**

I like painting.   He likes painting.

10 CD2 41 Sing the song.

Do you like ?
No, I don't. No, I don't.
Do you like ?
Yes, I do. Yes, I do.
I like !

Does he like ?
No, he doesn't. No, he doesn't.
Does he like ?
Yes, he does. Yes, he does.
He likes !

Do you like ?
No, I don't. No, I don't.
Do you like ?
Yes, I do. Yes, I do.
I like !

Does she like ?
No, she doesn't. No, she doesn't.
Does she like ?
Yes, she does. Yes, she does.
She likes !

11 CD2 42 Think Listen and say the number.

Grammar: *Do you like flying a kite?* **73**

1

Are you OK, David?

It's a basketball!

2

The *All Stars* are my favorite team!

Let's play! Put on these shirts!

3

That's not fair!

Play nicely, iPal.

4

I'm sorry.

That's OK.

5

Watch me! Throw the ball like this.

Yes!

6

Good job, Olivia!

Thanks, iPal.

74 Value: Play nicely

→ Workbook page 60

Listen and act.

Animal sounds

14 Listen and say.

A **c**amel with
a **c**amera.
A **k**angaroo
with a **k**ite.

What equipment do we need?

1 CD2 48 Listen and say.

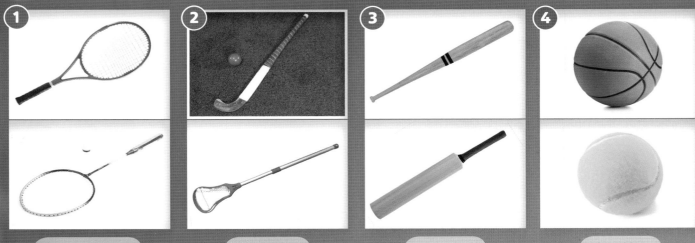

rackets   sticks   bats   balls

2 Watch the video.

3 Look and say *racket*, *stick*, *bat*, or *ball*.

Number 1. Ball.   Yes!

Guess What!

Project

4 Make a Carroll diagram.

Review Units 5 and 6

1 **Look and say the words.**

> Number 1. Fly a kite.

2 CD2 49 **Listen and say the color.**

Sue

Dan

→ Workbook pages 64–65

3 Play the game.

Start

Finish

79

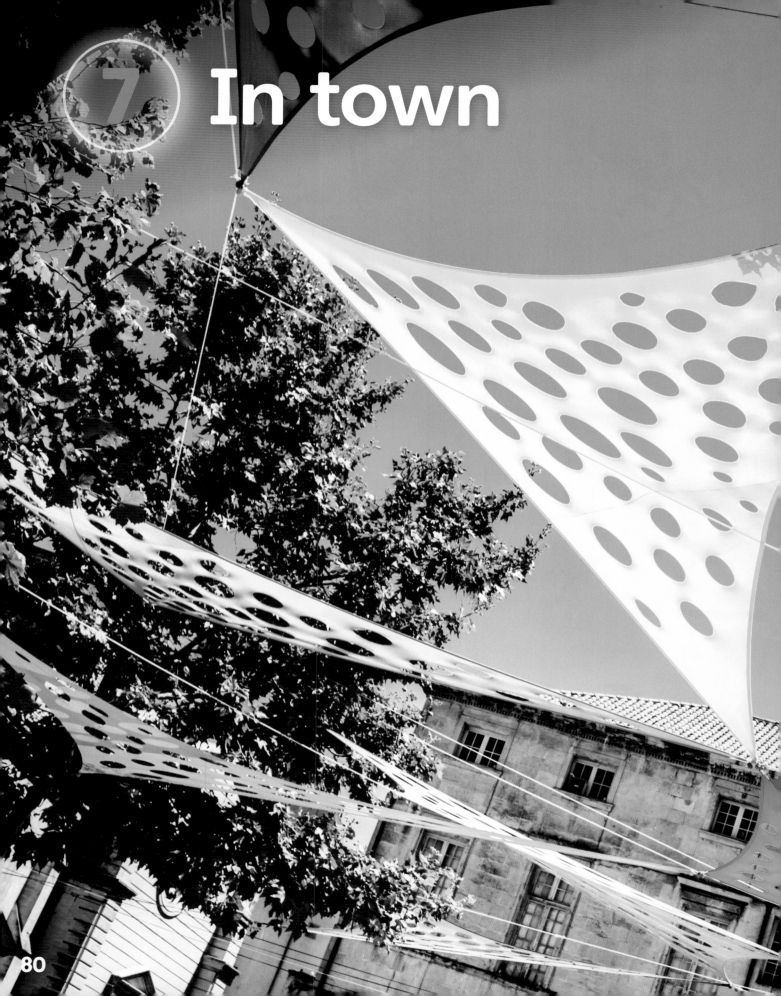

7 In town

Guess What!

8

1 CD3 02 Listen. Who's speaking?

2 CD3 03 Listen, point, and say.

1 park

2 movie theater

MOVIE THEATER

Now Showing: **Robots From Outer S**

3 clothing store

4 café

5 toy store

6 bookstore

7 supermarket

8 street

9 school

10 playground

3 CD3 04 Listen and find.

Find Leo

4 CD3 05 **Say the chant.**

sister

Come with me and look around.
Who's in the café in the town?
It's my sister! She's in the café.
She's in the café in the town.

brother

mom

dad

5 **Match and say.**

1, c. My cousin's on the playground.

a

b

1 My cousin's on the playground.
2 My aunt's in the clothing store.
3 My uncle's in the school.
4 My grandma's in the supermarket.
5 My grandpa's at the park.

c

d

e

6 Think **Think of a place. Say and guess.**

There's a desk and green chairs.

It's a school.

→ Workbook page 67

7 (CD3 07) **Sing the song.**

Come and visit my town,
My friendly little town.
It's nice to be in my town,
My little town.

There's a toy store and
a clothing store.
There's a bookstore
and a movie theater.
There's a café, and
there's a supermarket.
In my little town.

And the toy store is behind the
clothing store.
And the bookstore is in front of
the clothing store.
And the clothing store is between
the bookstore and the toy store!
In my little town.

And the movie theater is next to the café.
And the café is next to the supermarket.
And the café is between the supermarket
and the movie theater.

Come and visit my town ...

8 (CD3 08) **Look, listen, and find the mistakes.**

The movie theater is next to the supermarket.

No, it isn't. The movie theater is next to the café.

Listen, look, and say.

Is there a playground behind the school? Yes, there is.

Is there a café next to the movie theater? No, there isn't.

 Listen and say *yes* or *no*.

  Play the game.

Is there a café in front of the supermarket?

Yes, there is.

The movie theater is next to the school.

No, it isn't. The movie theater is next to the supermarket.

Grammar: *Is there a playground behind the school?* **85**

86 Value: Be safe

→ Workbook page 70

13   **Listen and act.**

Animal sounds

14 CD3 14 **Listen and say.**

A quick queen bee. An ox with an X-ray.

Where are the
places?

1 (CD3 16) **Listen and say.**

1

2

3

4

police station   fire station   hospital   sports center

2 **Watch the video.**

3 **Look and say the letter and number.**

A, 3.   Fire station.   Yes!

Guess What!

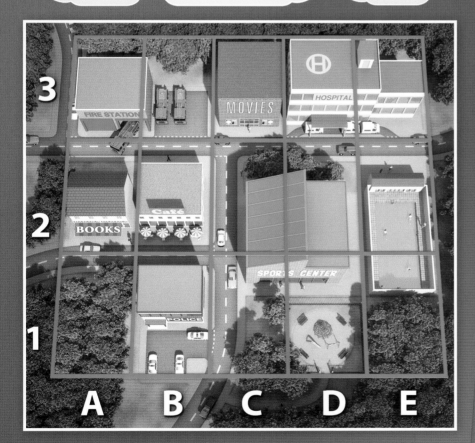

Project

4 **Draw a map of your town.**

8 On the farm

Guess What!

1 CD3 17 **Listen. Who's speaking?**

2 CD3 18 **Listen, point, and say.**

Café and Gift Store

1 field
2 barn
3 horse
4 donkey
5 sheep
6 goat
7 cow
8 duck
9 pond

3 CD3 19 **Listen and find.**

Find Leo

Say the chant.

donkey

Where's the donkey?
It's in the barn.
It's in the barn.
On the farm.

Where are the goats?
They're in the field.
They're in the field.
On the farm.

cow

goats

ducks

5 **Read and follow. Then ask and answer.**

Where's the cow?   It's in the field.

a

1 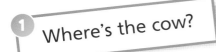 Where's the cow?

2 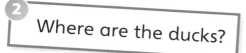 Where are the ducks?

b

3 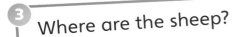 Where are the sheep?

4  Where's the horse?

c

6   **Ask and answer.**

What's your favorite animal?   It's a sheep.

7 CD3 22 Sing the song.

Field and pond, house and barn,

Look at the animals on the farm …

What's the doing?

It's swimming. It's swimming.

It's swimming.

What's the doing?

It's swimming in the .

Field and pond …

What's the doing?

It's running. It's running. It's running.

What's the doing?

It's running in the .

Field and pond …

What's the doing?

It's sleeping. It's sleeping.

It's sleeping.

What's the doing?

It's sleeping in the .

Field and pond …

What's the doing?

It's eating. It's eating. It's eating.

What's the doing?

It's eating in the .

Field and pond …

8 CD3 23 Listen and answer the questions.

 What's the duck doing? 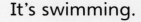 It's swimming.

1

2

3

4

5

6

7

8

9 CD3 24 Listen, look, and say.

1 Is the cat sleeping?   Yes, it is.

2 Is the duck swimming?   No, it isn't. It's flying.

10 Think Play the game.

Is the dog running?   Yes, it is.

Picture 1!

① It's a message for iPal.

Let's find him!

② Would you like to come to a party?

Yes, please!

③ Hold on!

We're flying!

④ Welcome to the party!

It's so nice to see you!

WELCOME HOME

⑤ What's Ben doing?

He's ... dancing!

⑥ Goodbye, iPal!

Goodbye! Thanks for taking care of me!

CD3 28 **Listen and act.**

Animal sounds

13 **CD3 29** Listen and say.

A wolf in the water.
A white whale with a wheel.

Functional language: *Would you like to come to my party?*
Pronunciation: *w, wh* **97**

What do **farmers** do?

1 CD3 31 Listen and say.

plant seeds

turn soil

water plants

harvest plants

2 Watch the video.

3 Look and say.

Number 1. He turns soil.   Yes!

Guess What!

Project

4 Draw how farmers grow our food.

Review Units 7 and 8

1 **Look and say the words.**

Number 1. Café.

 1

 2

 3

 4

 5

 6

 7

 8

2 **CD3 32** **Listen and say the name.**

Grace

Lola

Kento

Dan

→ Workbook pages 82–83

3 **Ask and answer.**

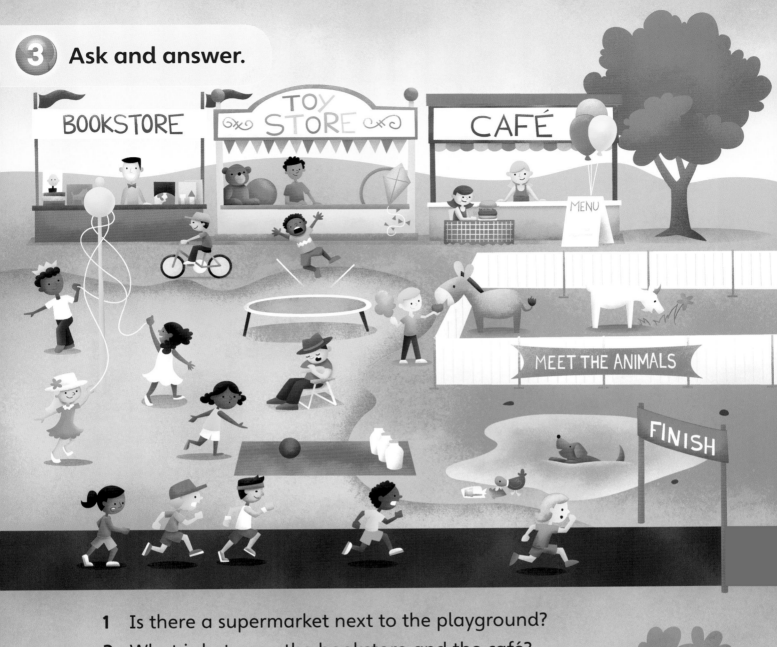

1 Is there a supermarket next to the playground?
2 What is between the bookstore and the café?
3 Is there a pond at the park?
4 What is the duck doing?
5 Is the dog sleeping?
6 What is the donkey doing?
7 Is she eating cereal?
8 What's he doing?
9 Is she swimming?
10 What's he doing?

My sounds

seal • zebra

camel • kangaroo

queen bee • ox

wolf • whale

Workbook 2B
with Online Resources

Contents

Susan Rivers

Series Editor: Lesley Koustaff

CAMBRIDGE
UNIVERSITY PRESS

5 Meals

1 Find and circle. Look and write the word.

1

rice

2

_____

3

_____

4

_____

5

_____

6

_____

peascarrotscerealricetoastfish

2 Look, read, and write *yes* or *no*.

1 There's meat on the table.
   _____yes_____

2 There are peas on the table.
   _____

3 There are potatoes on the table. _____

4 There are sausages on the table. _____

5 There's cereal on the table.
   _____

3 CD2 23 **Listen and stick.**

1

2

3

4

5

4 Think **Look and write the words.**

~~toast~~   cereal   peas   rice   meat
fish   sausages   potatoes   carrots

These foods are plants.	These foods aren't plants.

toast	

My picture dictionary → Go to page 84: Check the words you know and trace.

Vocabulary **49**

5 Listen and match. Draw a happy face or a sad face.

6 Look, read, and circle the words.

She **(likes)** / **doesn't** like fish.

He **likes** / **doesn't like** cereal.

She **likes** / **doesn't like** meat.

He **likes** / **doesn't like** peas.

7 **Look, read, and circle the words. Then answer the questions.**

Kim

Jim

1 Does Kim like (cereal) / **sausages**?
  Yes, she does.

2 Does Kim like **toast** / **peas**?
  No, she doesn't.

3 Does Kim like toast, for breakfast?
  Yes, she does.

4 Does Kim like sausages?
  _____

1 Does Jim like **carrots** / **potatoes**?
  Yes, he does.

2 Does Jim like **steak** / **fish**?
  No, he doesn't.

3 Does Jim like steak, for lunch?
  _____

4 Does Jim like potatoes?
  _____

8 **Draw and say. Then write and circle.**

My mom likes meat and carrots for dinner. She doesn't like fish.

My _____ likes _____ and _____
for dinner. He/She doesn't like _____ .

9 CD2 29 **Look and write the words. Then listen and check.**

| likes | fish | please | ~~lunch~~ | peas | Cake |

1. Look! Café Hawaii!

Café Hawaii

Let's go for _lunch_ !

2. Would you like _____ and potatoes?

Café Hawaii

Yes, please!

No, thank you!

3. What about carrots or _____ , iPal?

No, thank you!

4. Oh, dear! What would you like, iPal?

_____ ! I like chocolate cake.

5. More cake, _____ !

No, iPal. That's enough!

6. What's the matter?

He _____ chocolate cake – a lot!

10 **Look, read, and stick.**

I eat healthy food.

11 **Trace the letters.**

A seal in the sun. A zebra in the zoo.

12 CD2 32 **Listen and circle s or z.**

1

Ⓢ z

2

s z

3

s z

4

s z

What kind of **food** is it?

1 Look and write the words in the chart.

peas   sausages   rice   carrots

fish   cheese   milk   bread

fruits and vegetables	meat and fish	grains and cereals	dairy
peas			

Evaluation

1 **Read and write the word.**

1 T o a s t is bread.
2 C _ _ _ _ _ _ _ are orange. They come from plants.
3 F _ _ _ live in water. They can swim.
4 P _ _ _ are very small and green. They come from plants.
5 Chicken and sausages are m _ _ _ _ .
6 R _ _ _ is small and white. It comes from plants.

2 **What's your favorite part? Use your stickers.**

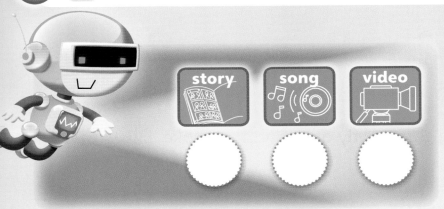

3 Puzzle **What's different? Circle and write.**
Then go to page 88 and write the letters.

_ _ _ _ _ _
7

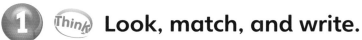

Activities

1 (Think) **Look, match, and write.**

 1
 2
 3
 4

a

ride a _____

b

play _____

c

fly a _____

d

take *photographs*

2 **Look and write the words.**

~~play~~   take   ride   fly   play   roller-skate

 1

A: Let's play tennis. Can you *play* tennis?

B: No, I can't, but I can _____ basketball.

 2

A: Can you _____ a horse?

B: Yes, I can, and I can _____ a kite, too.

 3

A: I can roller-skate. Can you _____?

B: No, I can't, but I can _____ photographs!

Listen and stick.

  Look and write the words.

| ride a horse | ~~play basketball~~ | play tennis |
| roller-skate | take photographs | play baseball |

play basketball

My picture dictionary **Go to page 85: Check the words you know and trace.**

Look at the chart. Circle the words and write.

	May	Tom	Jill	Sam
✓ **like**	fly a kite	play basketball	play baseball	roller-skate
✗ **don't like**	play tennis	play field hockey	ride a horse	take photographs

1
> I **like / don't like** playing tennis.

2
> I **like / don't like** playing field hockey.

3
> I **like / don't like** riding a horse.

4
> I **like / don't like** taking photographs.

5 May _____likes_____ flying a kite.

6 Tom _____ playing basketball.

7 Jill _____ playing baseball.

8 Sam _____ roller-skating.

6 **Look, read, and circle the answers.**

1

Do you like taking photographs?

(Yes, I do.) / No, I don't.

2

Do you like playing tennis?

Yes, I do. / No, I don't.

3

Does he like playing baseball?

Yes, he does. / No, he doesn't.

4

Does she like flying a kite?

Yes, she does. / No, she doesn't.

7 (About Me) **Complete the chart. Ask and answer.**

Do you like riding a horse?

Yes, I do.

No, I don't.

Do you like ...	riding a horse?	_____ ?	_____ ?
1 Me	yes / no	yes / no	yes / no
2 _____	yes / no	yes / no	yes / no
3 _____	yes / no	yes / no	yes / no

I like ...

_____ likes ...

9 Look, unscramble, and stick.

I (lypa) _____ nicely.

10 Trace the letters.

A camel with a camera. A kangaroo with a kite.

11 CD2 47 Listen and number the pictures.

a
 ☐

b
 ☐

c
 ☐

d
 ☐

e
 1

f
 ☐

What equipment do we need?

1 **Look and match the pictures.**

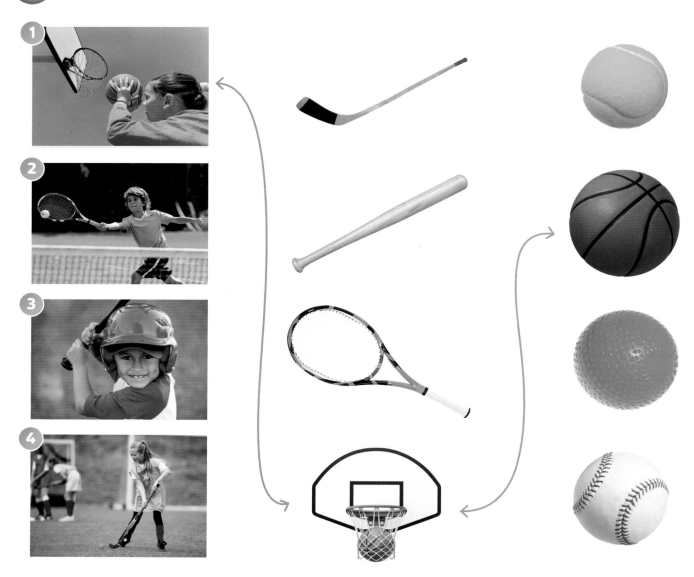

2 **Look at Activity 1 and write the words.**

1 I play basketball with a _____basket_____ and a _____ball_____ .
2 I play tennis with a _____ and a _____ .
3 I play baseball with a _____ and a _____ .
4 I play field hockey with a _____ and a _____ .

Evaluation

1 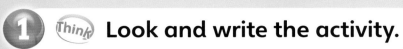 **Look and write the activity.**

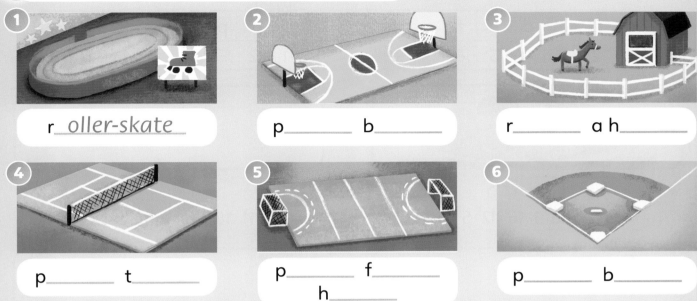

1 r _oller-skate_

2 p_____ b_____

3 r_____ a h_____

4 p_____ t_____

5 p_____ f_____ h_____

6 p_____ b_____

2 **What's your favorite part? Use your stickers.**

story   song   video

3 **Puzzle** **What's different? Circle and write.**
Then go to page 88 and write the letters.

___ ___ ___ ___ ___ ___ ___ ___ ___
      4   2

Review Units 5 and 6

1 Write and draw.

a	b	c	d	e	f	g	h	i	k	l	o	p	r	s	t	u	y
1	2	3	4	5	6	7	8	9	10	11	12	13	14	15	16	17	18

1

p o t a t o e s
13 12 16 1 16 12 5 15

2

_ _ _ _ _ _ _ _
6 11 18 1 10 9 16 5

3

_ _ _ _ _ _ _ _
15 1 17 15 1 7 5 15

4

_ _ _ _ _ _ _ _ _ _ _ _ _
13 11 1 18 2 1 15 10 5 16 2 1 11 11

5

_ _ _ _ _ _
3 5 14 5 1 11

6

_ _ _ _ _ _ - _ _ _ _ _
14 12 11 11 5 14 15 10 1 16 5

2 Read and match.

1	He likes		a	field hockey.
2	She doesn't		b	beans.
3	Does he		c	taking photographs?
4	I like playing		d	toast.
5	He doesn't like		e	like playing tennis?
6	Do you like		f	like meat.

64

3 Look, read, and write the words.

roller-skating   rice   ~~photographs~~   fish   ~~do~~   doesn't   does   don't

1

Do you like taking _photographs_ ?
Yes, I ___do___ .

2

Does she like _____ ?
Yes, she _____ .

3

Does he like _____ ?
No, he _____ .

4

Do you like _____ ?
No, I _____ .

4 Listen and check ✓.

CD2 50

1

2

In town

1 **Look at the picture and write the letter.**

1 street ___e___		**2** café _____	
3 school _____		**4** bookstore _____	
5 playground _____		**6** supermarket _____	

2 **Look at Activity 1 and write *yes* or *no*.**

1 There's a toy store in the town.   _no_

2 There's a playground in the town.   _____

3 There's a movie theater in the town.   _____

4 There's a café in the town.   _____

5 There's a clothing store in the town.   _____

6 There's a school in the town.   _____

Listen and stick.

1

2

3

4

5

 Think **Look and write.**

1

toy store

2

3

4

My picture dictionary → Go to page 86: Check the words you know and trace.

Look, read, and match.

1 next to

2 in front of

3 behind

4 between

6 **Look, read, and circle the words.**

1 The school is **behind** / (**next to**) the playground.

2 The toy store is **in front of** / **between** the bookstore and the clothing store.

3 The tree is **next to** / **in front of** the movie theater.

4 The supermarket is **behind** / **between** the park.

7 **Draw and say. Then write.**

My school is next to the park.

My school is _____

_____ .

8 **Look, read, and check ✓.**

1   Is there a toy store next to the school?
    Yes, there is. ☐   No, there isn't. ✓

2   Is there a café in front of the supermarket?
    Yes, there is. ☐   No, there isn't. ☐

3   Is there a toy store between the bookstore and the school?
    Yes, there is. ☐   No, there isn't. ☐

4   Is there a playground behind the school?
    Yes, there is. ☐   No, there isn't. ☐

9 **Complete the questions and the answers.**

1   _____Is there_____ a park next to the bookstore?
    No, _____there isn't_____ .

2   _____ a playground between the school
    and the supermarket?
    No, _____ .

3   _____ a street in front of the café?
    Yes, _____ .

4   _____ a park behind the supermarket?
    Yes, _____ .

10 CD3 12 Read and write the letter. Then listen and check.

a No, iPal! Be careful!

b I like going to the movies.

c Movie tickets!

d Oh, no! It's closed today!

e Look left and right.

f Where's the movie theater?

1 c

They're from my cousin, Anna!

2 It's next to the supermarket.

3 Let's go!

4 It's safe now. Let's cross.

5 Come with me!

6 It's a movie about robots!

11 Look, unscramble, and stick.

I am (esfa) _____ .

12 Trace the letters.

A quick queen bee. An ox with an X-ray.

13 CD3 15 Listen and write *qu* or *x*.

1

_qu_ een bee

2

6

si__

3

o__

4

____ick

Where are the places?

1 Look, read, and circle the word.

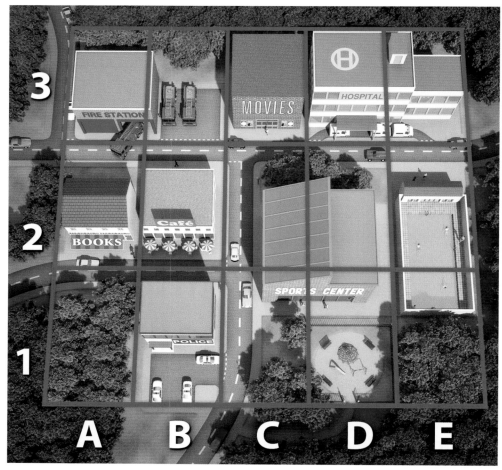

1 There's a (fire station) / **police station** in A3.

2 There's a **movie theater** / **bookstore** in C3.

3 There's a **café** / **hospital** in B2.

4 There's a **movie theater** / **bookstore** in C3.

2 Look at Activity 1 and answer the questions.

1 Where's the police station? _____B1_____

2 Where's the bookstore? _____

3 Where's the hospital? _____

4 Where's the sports center? _____

Evaluation

1 Think **Look and write the word.**

1. supermarket
2. _____
3. _____
4. _____
5. _____
6. _____

2 **What's your favorite part? Use your stickers.**

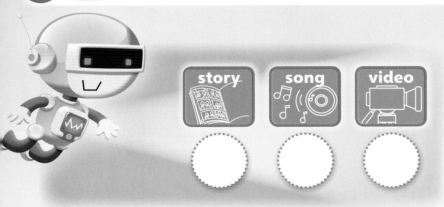

story   song   video

3 Puzzle **What's different? Circle and write.**
Then go to page 88 and write the letters.

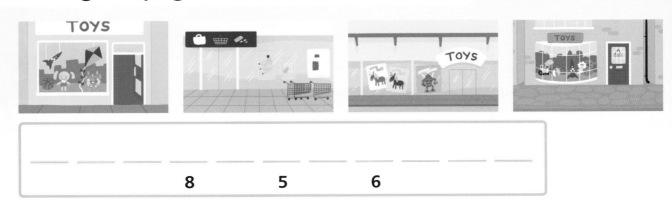

TOYS   TOYS   TOYS

_____

8   5   6

8 On the farm

1 Look, read, and circle the word.

cow / horse

sheep / goat

barn / field

horse / donkey

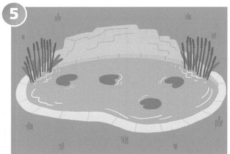

field / pond

duck / donkey

2 Follow the animal words.

Start →

cow	goat	park	barn
field	duck	sheep	air
hospital	grains	donkey	school
dairy	pond	cat	horse

Good job!

3 CD3 21 Listen and stick.

1

2

3

4

5

4 Think **Read and write the word.**

1 Milk comes from this animal. It isn't a goat.   _____cow_____

2 This animal can swim and fly. It likes water.   _____

3 We can ride this animal. It's not a donkey.   _____

4 Wool comes from this animal.   _____

5 This is a house for cows and horses.   _____

6 Fish and ducks swim in this.   _____

My picture dictionary → Go to page 87: Check the words you know and trace.

5 **Look, read, and check ✓.**

1

The cow is eating.	✓
The cow is jumping.	☐

2

The horse is running.	☐
The horse is sleeping.	☐

3

The duck is flying.	☐
The duck is swimming.	☐

6 **Look, read, and answer the questions.**

1

What's the donkey doing?

It's eating.

2

What's the duck doing?

_____

3

What's the goat doing?

_____

4

What's the sheep doing?

_____

7 (About Me) **Draw your favorite farm animal. Then write.**

This is a _____ .
It's _____ .

8 **CD3 25 Listen and check ✓ or put an ✗.**

1
 ✓

2
 ☐

3
 ☐

4
 ☐

9 **Look, read, and circle the word.**

1

Is the horse **eating** / (sleeping) ?
No, it isn't.

2

Is the cow **running** / **sleeping**?
Yes, it is.

3

Is the goat **sleeping** / **jumping**?
No, it isn't.

4

Is the duck **swimming** / **flying**?
Yes, it is.

5

Is the sheep **eating** / **running**?
No, it isn't.

6

Is the horse **sleeping** / **swimming**?
No, it isn't.

party   ~~iPal~~   dancing   Goodbye   flying   Welcome

1 It's a message for ___iPal___ . Let's find him!

2 Would you like to come to a _____ ? Yes, please!

3 Hold on! We're _____ !

4 _____ to the party! It's so nice to see you! WELCOME HOME iPAL

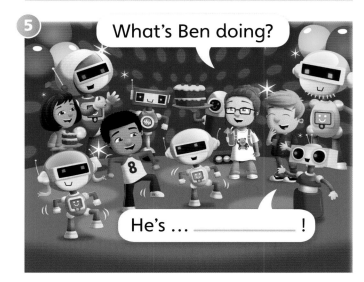

5 What's Ben doing? He's … _____ !

6 _____ , iPal! Goodbye! Thanks for taking care of me!

11 Look, unscramble, and stick.

I love my (ehmo) _____ .

12 Trace the letters.

A wolf in the water.
A white whale with
a wheel.

13 CD3 30 Listen and put a check ✓ next to *w* or *wh*.

1	w ✓	wh ☐	2	w ☐	wh ☐
3	w ☐	wh ☐	4	w ☐	wh ☐

What do farmers do?

1 Look and number the pictures.

2 Look at Activity 1 and write the letter.

1 A farmer turns soil. | b |

2 A farmer plants seeds. | |

3 A farmer waters plants. | |

4 A farmer harvests plants. | |

Evaluation

1 **Write the words and find.**

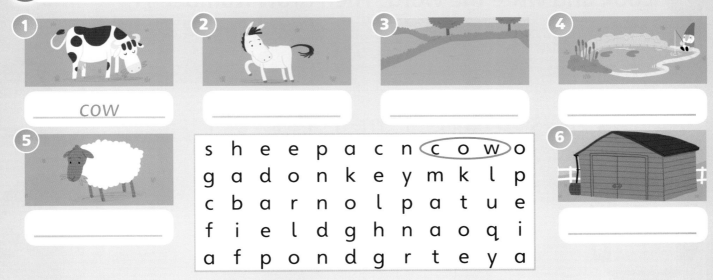

1. COW
2.
3.
4.
5.
6.

```
s h e e p a c n (c o w) o
g a d o n k e y m k l p
c b a r n o l p a t u e
f i e l d g h n a o q i
a f p o n d g r t e y a
```

2 **What's your favorite part? Use your stickers.**

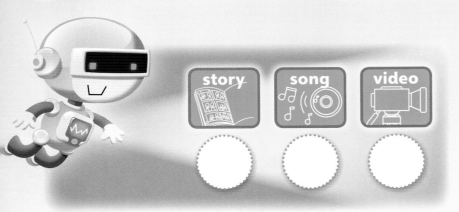

story   song   video

3 **Puzzle** **What's different? Circle and write. Then go to page 88 and write the letters.**

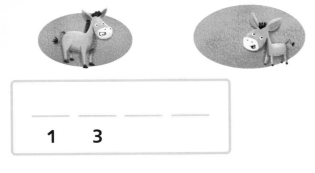

1 ___ 3 ___

Review Units 7 and 8

1 Look and write the word. Then draw Number 11.

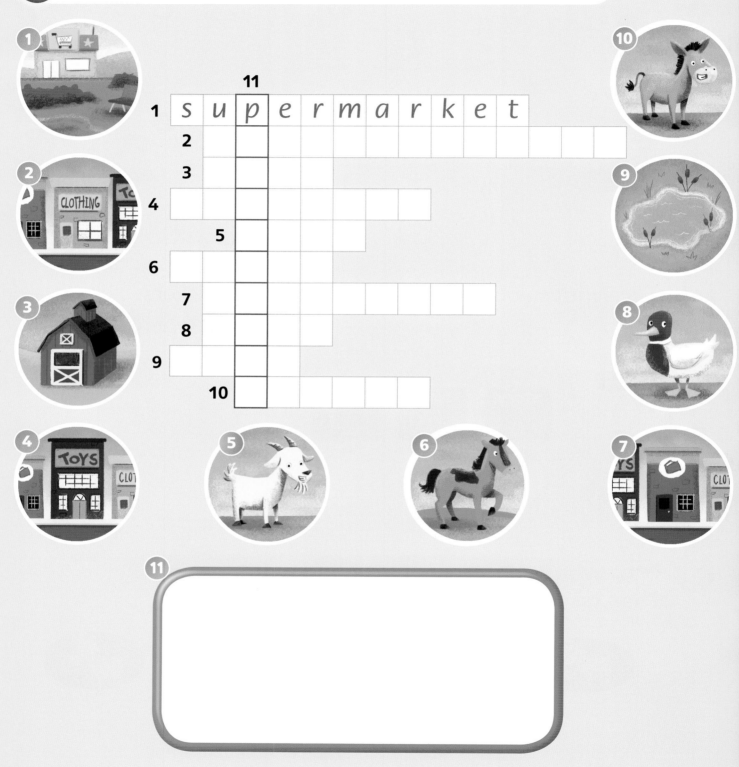

1 | s | u | p | e | r | m | a | r | k | e | t

11

2

3

4

5

6

7

8

9

10

82

2 Look, read, and write the answers.

1

What's the goat doing?

It's jumping.

2

Is there a park next to
the supermarket?

_____

3

Is the sheep running?

_____

4

What's the horse doing?

_____

3 Listen and check ✓.

1

2

83

5 Meals

beans

carrots

cereal

fish

meat

peas

potatoes

rice

sausages

toast

6 Activities

fly a kite ☐

play baseball ☐

play basketball ☐

play field hockey ☐   take photographs ☐

ride a horse ☐   roller-skate ☐   play tennis ☐

7 In town

bookstore

café

movie theater

clothing store

park

play- ground

school

street

supermarket

toy store

8 On the farm

barn

cow

donkey

duck

field

goat

horse

pond

sheep

My puzzle

1 Write the letters in the correct place.

_ _ _ _ JOB, _ Y F _ _ _ ND!
1 2 3 4   5   6 7 8

Thanks and Acknowledgements

Many thanks to everyone in the excellent team at Cambridge University Press. In particular we would like to thank Emily Hird, Liane Grainger, and Flavia Lamborghini whose professionalism, enthusiasm, experience, and talent makes them all such a pleasure to work with.

We would also like to give special thanks to Lesley Koustaff for her unfailing support, expert guidance, good humor, and welcome encouragement throughout the project.

The authors and publishers would like to thank the following contributors:
Blooberry Design: concept design, cover design, book design, page makeup
Emma Szlachta, Vicky Bewick: editing
Lisa Hutchins: freelance editing
Ann Thomson: art direction, picture research
Gareth Boden: commissioned photography
Jon Barlow: commissioned photography
Ian Harker: audio recording
Robert Lee, Dib Dib Dub Studios: song and chant composition
Vince Cross: theme tune composition
James Richardson: arrangement of theme tune
John Marshall Media: audio recording and production
Phaebus: video production
hyphen S.A.: publishing management, American English edition

The authors and publishers acknowledge the following sources of copyright material and are grateful for the permissions granted. Although every effort has been made, it has not always been possible to identify the sources of all the material used or to trace all copyright holders.

If any omissions are brought to our notice, we will be happy to include the appropriate acknowledgments on reprinting.

The authors and publishers would like to thank the following illustrators:

Student's Book
Marek Jagucki, pp59, 60, 64, 69, 70, 74, 81, 82, 86, 91, 92, 96; Kirsten Collier (Bright Agency), pp65, 75, 87, 97, 102; Andy Parker, pp89; Joelle Dreidemy (Bright Agency), pp61, 83; Woody Fox (Bright Agency), pp62, 73, 84; Richard Watson (Bright Agency), pp63, 95; Marcus Cutler (Sylvie Poggio), pp79, 101

Workbook
Barbara Bakos (Bright Agency) 59, 65, 73, 76, 83; Gareth Conway (Bright Agency) 65, 67, 69, 73, 74, 81; Humberto Blanco (Sylvie Poggio Agency) 58, 68, 76; Kimberley Barnes (Bright Agency) 63, 68; Lucy Fleming (Bright Agency) 61, 71, 79; Marcus Cutler (Sylvie Poggio Agency) 63, 64, 66, 68, 81, 82; Marek Jagucki 60, 61, 63, 70, 71, 73, 74, 78, 81, 88, stickers; Monkey Feet 84, 85, 86, 87; Phil Garner (Beehive Illustration) 77, 83; Andy Parker 72; Kirsten Collier (Bright Agency) 61, 71, 79

The authors and publishers would like to thank the following for permission to reproduce photographs:

Student's Book
p.58–59: Naho Yoshizawa/Shutterstock; p.63 (Tony): Craig Richardson/Alamy5; p.63 (Kim): Tracy Whiteside/Alamy; p.63 (Tom): Blend Images/Alamy; p.63 (Pat): Tracy Whiteside/Alamy; p.63 (meat): Jacek Chabraszewski/Shutterstock; p.63 (fish): Eskymaks/Shutterstock; p.63 (potatoes): Kevin Mayer/Shutterstock; p.63 (carrots): Maria Komar/Shutterstock; p.63 (rice): oriori/Shutterstock; p.63 (beans): mayer kleinostheim/Shutterstock; p.63 (toast): alnavegante/Shutterstock; p.65 (B/G), p.97 (B/G): Jolanta Wojcicka/Shutterstock; p.65 (T): Andrew Olney/Shutterstock; p.66–67: Stefano Politi Markovina/Alamy; p.67 (T-1): matka_Wariatka/Shutterstock; p.67 (T-2): sarsmis/Shutterstock; p.67 (T-3): Jag_cz/Shutterstock; p.67 (T-4): Christine Langer-Pueschel/Shutterstock; p.67 (T-5): Christian Draghici/Shutterstock; p.67 (B-1): koss13/Shutterstock; p.67 (B-2): Christian Jung/Shutterstock; p.67 (B-3): Adam Gault/Getty Images; p.67 (B-4): Africa Studio/Shutterstock; p.68–69: Leander Baerenz/Getty Images; p.71 (baseball): Dan Thornberg/Shutterstock; p.71 (basketball): Aaron Amat/Shutterstock; p.71 (kite): Hurst Photo/Shutterstock; p.71 (horse): Alex White/Shutterstock; p.71 (camera): taelove7/Shutterstock; p.71 (skates), p.71 (e): J. Helgason/Shutterstock; p.71 (a): gorillaimages/Shutterstock; p.71 (b): Veronica Louro/Shutterstock; p.71 (c): Ramona Heim/Shutterstock; p.71 (d): Rob Bouwman/Shutterstock; p.72 (C): Hybrid Images/Getty Images; p.72 (CR): Production Perig/Shutterstock; p.72 (CL): racorn/Shutterstock; p.72 (BL): auremar/Shutterstock; p.72 (BR): Kuttig – People/Alamy; p.75 (T): F1online digitale Bildagentur GmbH/Alamy; p.76–77: 13/David Madison/Ocean/Corbis; p.77 (T-1); p.77 (T-2): Image Source Plus/Alamy; p.77 (T-3): onilmilk/Shutterstock; p.77 (T-4): Aaron Amat/Shutterstock; p.77 (rackets): anaken2012/Shutterstock; p.77 (sticks): Bill Frische/Shutterstock; p.77 (bats): Sean Gladwell/Shutterstock; p.77 (balls): mexrix/Shutterstock; p.77 (B-1): Pal2iyawit/Shutterstock; p.77 (B-2): Ian Buchan/Shutterstock; p.77 (B-3): isitsharp/Getty Images; p.77 (B-4): Visionhaus/Corbis; p.78 (1): Fir4ik/Shutterstock; p.78 (2): Ledo/Shutterstock; p.78 (3): Nattika/Shuterstock; p.78 (4): Ramon grosso dolarea/Shutterstock; p.78 (5): Tischenko Irina/Shutterstock; p.78 (6): igor.stevanovic/Shutterstock; p.78 (7): Joe Gough/Shutterstock; p.78 (8): Elnur/Shutterstock; p.78 (Sue): Tracy Whiteside/Shutterstock; p.78 (Dan): oliveromg/Shutterstock; p.78 (BC skates): StockPhotosArt/Shutterstock; p.78 (BC hockey): Leonid Shcheglov/Shutterstock; p.78 (BL): Igor Dutina/Shutterstock; p.78 (BR): Lauri Patterson/Getty Images; p.80–81: Peter Burnett/Getty Images; p.83 (TL): Gladskikh Tatiana/Shutterstock; p.83 (brother): Pavel L Photo and Video/Shutterstock; p.83 (mom): racorn/Shutterstock; p.83 (dad): Carlos Yudica/Shutterstock; p.87 (B/G): AAMNF3/Alamy; p.87 (T): Adrian Sherratt/Alamy; p.88: A.P.S.(UK)/Alamy; p.89 (1): meunierd/Alamy; p.89 (2): Sava Alexandru/Getty; p. 89 (3): Rosalrene Betancourt 5/Alamy; p.89 (4): Mike Robinson/Alamy; p.90–91: Getty Images; p.93 (TL): Dieter Hawlan/Shutterstock; p.93 (TR): Orhan Cam/Shutterstock; p.93 (CL): Sebastian Knight/Shutterstock; p.93 (CR): Isantilli/Shutterstock; p.93 (a): American Spirit/Shutterstock; p.93 (b): Scott Prokop/Shutterstock; p.93 (c): Brian Goodman/Shutterstock; p.94 (B/G): Dudarev Mikhail/Shutterstock; p.94 (horse): Lenkadan/Shutterstock; p.94 (field): robert_s/Shutterstock; p.94 (duck): Geanina Bechea/Shutterstock; p.94 (pond): Yuriy Kulik/Shutterstock; p.94 (cat): Rumo/Shutterstock; p.94 (house): bbofdon/Shutterstock; p.94 (cow): jesadaphorn/Shutterstock; p.94 (barn): Bonita R. Cheshier/Shutterstock; p.94 (1): Diane Picard/Shutterstock; p.94 (2): Schubbel/Shutterstock; p.94 (3): Ewa Studio/Shutterstock; p.94 (4): Michael Durham/Getty Images; p.94 (5): Makarova Viktoria/Shutterstock; p.94 (6): Kemeo/Shutterstock; p.94 (7): Ballawless/Shutterstock; p.94 (8): Alexander Matvienko/Alamy; p.98–99: Stephen Dorey/Getty Images; p.99 (1): Danylo Saniylenko/Shutterstock; p.99 (2): Tim Scrivener/Alamy; p.99 (3): Keith Dannemiller/Corbis; p.99 (4): Alex Treadway/National Geographic Society/Corbis; p.100 (1): Shchipkova Elena/Shutterstock; p100 (2): Arterra Picture Library/Alamy; p.100 (3): THPStock/Shutterstock; p.100 (4): Brandon Seidel/Shutterstock; p.100 (5): 1stGallery/Shutterstock; p.100 (6): Denise Lett/Shutterstock; p.100 (7): imageBROKER/Alamy; p.100 (8): IxMaster/Shutterstock; p.100 (CL): Blend Images/Alamy; p.100 (CR), p.100 (BR): imageBROKER/Alamy; p.100 (BL): Alinute Silzeviciute/Shutterstock.

Commissioned photography by Gareth Boden: p.67 (BR), p.77 (BR), p.89 (BR), p.99 (BR); Jon Barlow: p.61, p.62, p.71 (T), p.72 (TL), p.72 (TR), p.72 (BC), p.85, p.95 (B), p. 97 (T).

Workbook
p.62 (Unit Header): ©13/David Madison/Ocean/Corbis; p.62 (1L): ©zefart/Shutterstock; p.62 (2L): ©Juergen Hasenkopf/Alamy; p.62 (3L): ©Digital Media Pro/Shutterstock; p.62 (4L): ©redsnapper/Alamy; p.62 (1R): ©irin-k/Shutterstock; p.62 (2R): ©Lightspring/Shutterstock; p.62 (3R): ©peterboxy/Shutterstock; p.62 (4R): ©Dan Thornberg/Shutterstock; p.62 (1C): Stockbyte/Getty Images; p.62 (2C): ©amstockphoto/Shutterstock; p.62 (3C): ©C-You/iStock/Getty Images Plus/Getty Images; p.62 (4C): ©Slavoljub Pantelic/Shutterstock; p.66 (Unit Header): ©Peter Burnett/Getty Images; p.72 (Unit Header): ©A.P.S.(UK)/Alamy; p.74 (Unit Header): ©Getty Images; p.80 (Unit Header): ©Stephen Dorey/Photolibrary/Getty Images; p.80 (a): ©xalanx/iStock/Getty Images Plus/Getty Images; p.80 (b): ©fotokostic/iStock /Getty Images Plus/Getty Images; p.80 (c): ©Echo/Cultura/Getty Images; p.80 (d): ©Maskot/Corbis.

Our special thanks to the following for their kind help during location photography:

Everyone Active-Parkside Pool Cambridge, Queen Emma primary School

Front Cover photo by Lynne Gilbert/Getty Images